MY COWBOY'S GIFT

a story of faith in poetry and song

adapted from
the stage play

*written by
Andy
Wilkinson*

Grey Horse Press

ISBN 1-888609-10-9

Copyright, 1998. All Rights Reserved
All songs © 1998, Cain't Quit Music, Inc. (BMI)

"My Cowboy's Gift" may not be performed, in whole or in part,
without the express, written permission of the author.

Grey Horse Press
612 Broadway
Lubbock, TX 79401

Telephone 806-740-0100
Facsimile 806-749-1866
www.grey-horse.com

Graphic Design by Hartsfield Design, Lubbock, Texas

FOREWORD

"My Cowboy's Gift" first appeared as a one-act drama for the stage, written and performed entirely in poetry and song. Owing, perhaps, to the condensed and concise nature of poetic language, a surprising number of the audience asked for copies of the script, which has prompted the adaptation of the play into book form. The process has been straightforward: the stage directions and lighting cues were simply eliminated, with the only concession to the piece's theatrical heritage being to identify the speakers and singers of the various poems and songs.

Set in the contemporary American west, "My Cowboy's Gift" is an exploration of acceptance; how, when hurled into that chasm between what we demand to know and what we are able to know by way of reason, we must undergo the metamorphosis of faith, a metamorphosis made possible by love. The story is that of a rancher who, while attending to his recently-deceased wife's personal effects, has found a cache of old poems, some written by his wife and some by a cowboy who worked at the ranch many years before. Growing fearful as he reads them, for it seems obvious that they are poems between lovers, the rancher thinks back over the years, fear turning to jealousy, jealousy to anger, anger to bewilderment, and, finally, bewilderment to dismay. He argues with himself about the facts and the meaning of the facts, re-hashing the past. As he speaks, the other characters—the wife's spirit, and the cowboy—appear and tell the story from their own points of view, in song and in poetry, sometimes together, sometimes alone. Though the rancher never acknowledges the presence of the other two, his story and theirs are intertwined, the song or poem of one character triggering that of another. It is through these poems and songs that the rancher ultimately achieves his metamorphosis.

A word about the title. On large spreads, where owners most often live elsewhere and day-to-day operations are done by employees, the top hired hand is usually called by the title of manager or foreman. On small ranches, the owner and the owner's family do most of the work. A few small ranches from time to time can afford a permanent hand, a man who lives on the ranch and draws full-time wages. But as short of titles as they are of capital, these small ranch owners generally refer to such a hand simply as "my cowboy" (as in, "I'll send my cowboy over to help you unload those steers"). In this piece, the cowboy is "my cowboy" to both the rancher, in the usage just described, and to the wife in a very different way. But "my cowboy's" gift is much the same to both rancher and wife; it is his poetic love of the wife that serves as catalyst to both rancher and wife to move each toward a complete understanding of themselves and a better understanding of the power and the practical requirement of love in human affairs.

Andy Wilkinson
Lubbock, Texas

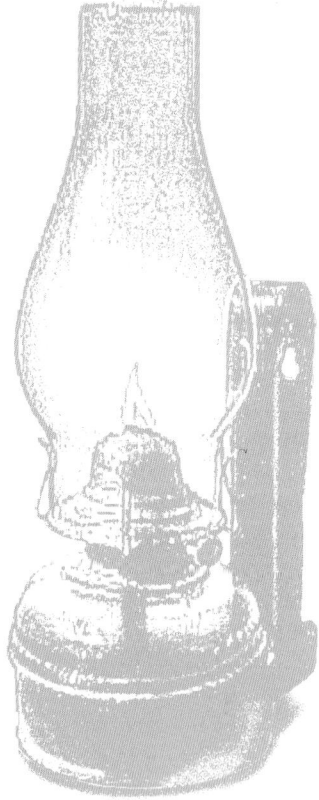

My Cowboy's Gift

The setting is the ambiguous present. It is late of an afternoon in the early fall, the sun throwing long shadows across the sitting porch on the head-quarters of a small ranch on the Texas plains. In the yard is a windmill.

The Three Voices belong to women of the community, contemporaries of the rancher and his wife. As they speak, the strains of "Amazing Grace" can be heard in the distance, played by a solitary fiddle.

It was so unexpected.   FIRST WOMAN'S VOICE

        Land sakes, girl!   SECOND WOMAN'S VOICE
It's always unexpected, dyin' is;
No matter death itself is certain sure,
A body can no more than hope to go
Some easy, some sorter quick-like. Let say,
Them preachers, all about them golden streets,
'Twon't be too many shakes the live-long dust
From off the welcome mat and holds the screen-door
Open to that angel dressed in black...

Especially them folks what never comes   THIRD WOMAN'S VOICE interrupts
To church. I 'spose the last time that we seen
Her husband in a pew was when they had
A sprinklin' for that baby boy of theirs,
An' that's been better than some thirty years.

But didn't she look natch'ral? Lord, she was   FIRST WOMAN'S VOICE
Always a beauty.

        Such a peaceful look,   SECOND WOMAN'S VOICE
All pillowed-up in all that satin fluff—
Her soul must have been saved!

          Well, maybe so,   THIRD WOMAN'S VOICE
But I'm a-thinkin' that she had to save
Her own soul. Got no help from that hard man.

The Rancher is an active man in his late middle age, queerly dressed for the time and place: bareheaded, a drab suit that never fit properly, the tie slipped loose, the waist coat fastened only at the top button, the pant legs haphazardly in the tops of well-worn hand-made boots. He carries a mismatched sheaf of papers, brought together by a ribbon.

The Rancher's Prologue

The kin, the friends, the wishers-well,
All have come and gone—
But I've a story yet to tell
In a poet's song
To an old man's metered stanza.
Though I'll weary soon,
It's warm here on the veranda
Come late afternoon
And I beg your helpful kindness,
Your ear, your advice:
Must truth turn to fact a blindness
Seeking paradise?
And how can justice come to be?
How turn right from wrong?
When those who gave the injury
To the past belong?

The Loosing of the Satin Twine

I have just come from burying my prize
Among the marker stones and cedar trees
Upon a slight and scruffy rocky rise,
The parson's Bible rippling in the breeze,
The women all in black, the men in ties
And suits and shoes, in knots of twos and threes,
The skirts held fast, the pants too high, the eyes
Down cast, the sky carved in a moving frieze
Of figures in a woeful enterprise
Who carried in a wooden box the ease
Of all my life: my wife, my right hand, wise
And beautiful, my partner, and my prize.

Perhaps I should have buried these the same,
These poems I found in her cedar chest
Bound-up in ribbon like a gift, her name
On half, another name on all the rest,
A name not mine, a name I could not claim
At first—my mind not clear, I was hard-pressed
To recollect a former beau, or flame
From youth, for poems so exchanged suggest
A romance 'tween the two. And then it came
To me: he was my cowboy, and the best
Who worked this ranch. Oh! never held I blame
For her on any count, 'til now. My breast
Grows heavy with the burden of the shame
These verses from the dead have just confessed.
Perhaps I should have buried them the same.

But, foolishly, I loosed this satin twine
And turned these poems out.
                        What's done is done,
There is no turning back the verse and line,
Once written, and once read. And what's begun
I'll end, the consequences only mine,
Except for this:
                        what will I tell my son?
What will I tell my son that won't malign
The image of his mother, with this one,
Quick, foolish loosing of a satin twine?

Making the Circle

They must have known one another
Many years before,
Not that I think they'd been lovers,
Though I can't be sure
For they seemed like old compadres
The moment they met,
Familiar in those private ways
I still can't forget:
The looks that lingered for moments
Longer than they should,
The too-careful phrases, the comments
Too quick understood.

But 'twas me who'd made the circle.
He was passin' through
And, needin' a good day-worker,
Thinkin' that he'd do,
I hired 'im to mend my fences,
Cut posts, dig the holes,
Never thinkin' consequences
Such work has on souls
When the boss man doesn't worry
The bad job well-turned
And allows no hand to curry
Favors rightly earned.

I'd have seen the clear credentials
Of the 'puncher tribe
If I'd measured his essentials,
Let my reckons gibe
With my horse-sense first impressions,
Those most often true,
For he set naught in possessions,
Just what he could do.

And I should've thought it funny
When he asked for work
That he never asked 'bout money
Nor would ever shirk
The least agreeable orders,
Just got on 'em quick,
Never behaved like a boarder,
Never begged-off sick.

Of his work, I made no mention,
Too busy for such,
And it isn't my convention
To carry-on much
When a man does what he's s'posed to,
But his case was clear,
By time we shipped, he's segundo,
Foreman, in a year.

The Cowboy is an age compatible with the events of the past. He is dressed in working cowboy attire: hat, chaps, work shirt, a brightly-colored wildrag, boots, and a pair of jingle-bob spurs. As with the rancher and the rancher's wife, he also carries a sheaf of papers, but different in appearance from the others.

THE COWBOY
sings

The Tribe of the Forty-and-Found

Don't worry my name
Whether for credit or blame;
Taking my measure
For trash or for treasure
Life is the handle I claim.

> I ride from the cowpuncher nation,
> The tribe of the forty-and-found,
> My life is a brave occupation,
> To range and to prairie I'm bound,
> A cowboy for forty-and-found.

You'll learn one thing that's true:
I don't work for money or you.
No cowboy gauges
His work by his wages
Doin' what he's born to do.

> I ride from the cowpuncher nation,
> The tribe of the forty-and-found,
> My life is a brave occupation,
> To range and to prairie I'm bound,
> A cowboy for forty-and-found.

4

I play in the Kingdom of Grass;
I pray at the houlihan mass;
I write my verses
In hard work and curses;
I sing with the luck that I pass.

> I ride from the cowpuncher nation,
> The tribe of the forty-and-found,
> My life is a brave occupation,
> To range and to prairie I'm bound,
> A cowboy for forty-and-found.

All She Had Forsworn

THE RANCHER
speaks

The foreman? Well, that's quite a stretch;
They's just me and him.
At brandin' time, I'd have to fetch
Day-work boys, like Slim
From up to Silverton, or Ben
From near to McLean,
And when the works were over, then
Send 'em home again
To bring 'em back, when it turned fall
And time came to ship.
But, most the year, we done it all,
Gave the Devil slip—

A-horseback, hard work life,
My cowboy and me.

Though, s'pose were I to count my wife,
That would then make three
Upon this prairie range-land croft,
'Cept when I was gone,
Which was, I now learn, once too oft,
Leavin' two alone.

Those years were mean and thin and tight.
While I worked the range,
She did her chorin', day and night,
Never seekin' change
Although it's some monotonous:
Me gone ever day
Then ridin' home late in a fuss
For the shortest stay—
Before the dawn, up, gone again,
The same, drab routine,
No matter sun or snow or rain
Or some inbetween.

Without a grumble, she'd get up,
Put the pot to heat,
Fry bacon, eggs, then fill my cup,
Sit and watch me eat,
Then wave good-bye as I rode out
To the dark-edged morn,
And never say a thing about
All she had forsworn.

The Rancher's Wife is a spirit, dressed in simple, rugged garments that are all in white. She carries a sheaf of papers identical to that of the rancher.

THE RANCHER'S
WIFE *sings*

Do You Know My Name

When death comes to quench the embers
That were once in flame,
Love runs true when love remembers
Where and whence it came.

> Don't look through me; you once knew me,
> Once, our hearts were the same;
> Wife or lover, goddess, mother—
> Do you know my name?
> Who else loved you like I loved you,
> Without reason or shame?
> Love's not clever, love's forever;
> Do you know my name?

Don't let justice bring false worry,
Love makes no such claim;
Love is trusting, love's not sorry,
Love seeks not for blame.

> Don't pass by me, don't deny me,
> Once, our lives were the same;
> Wife or lover, goddess, mother—
> Do you know my name?
> Who else loved you like I loved you,
> Without reason or shame?
> Love's not clever, love's forever;
> Do you know my name?

Love, I gave you, love to save you,
Love will love proclaim;
Child of beauty, child of duty,
Whether strong or lame.

Don't forget me, don't regret me,
We were one in the same;
Wife or lover, goddess, mother—
Do you know my name?
Who else loved you like I loved you,
Without reason or shame?
Love's not clever, love's forever;
Do you know my name?

Lanterns

THE RANCHER
speaks

She kept her counsel to herself,
Smiled, when she's addressed,
Kept all her troubles on the shelf,
Never once confessed
To feelin' punk or blue or sad
Or offered to whine,
Just knuckled down to good and bad,
Doin' at the time
What needed doin', never said
What's botherin' her,
If ever bother filled her head
Or put heart to spur.

She did have habits, though, that seemed
Peculiar to me:
She wrote down ever thing she dreamed
Into poetry
On paper bags, old envelopes,
Tied 'em with ribbons
And stored 'em in her chest of hopes
Like gifts t'were given
And gotten—
              that's where these were found,
Among those scribbles,
All careful laid, in bright silk bound—
And, too, she'd quibble
When I'd refer to them as verse;
Called 'em her "lanterns,"
And swore that each, for good or worse,
Was a light that burned.

7

The Journey's End

Not long ago, this trackless plain
Would test the trav'ler's skill;
An open, low, and bold terrain
With neither tree nor hill,

Nor graded road, nor gated fence
To break the line of sight;
By light of day, it was immense
And infinite, by night.

'Twas custom, then, at house or camp
When darkfall took the hour,
To hang a burning coal-oil lamp
Atop a windmill tower,

As gift to cowhands, bunkhouse bound,
To neighbors come to talk,
To strangers lost and strangers found,
To pilgrims on their walk.

No matter that it measured far
To where the lantern glowed,
That kerosene-fired windmill star
Put purpose to the road—

It was enough to see it flick
And know someone had toiled
To climb the 'mill and trim the wick
And keep the lantern oiled,

Not caring who'd be in its need,
Or who would seek it out—
The comfort in that selfless deed
Would ease the traveler's doubt.

Now, times have changed, and roads are paved
And marked by sign and post,
Still, there are travelers to be saved,
And, still, no fewer lost.

Today, my lamp is poetry,
Hung high upon the page,
Though burning, oh, so differently
The wandering to gauge,

Awaiting eyes to seek the names
Of spirits in the rhymes
Where once they sought the coal-oil flames
In stormed and darkened times,

And guiding in the manner of
The burning kerosene,
From far away, a gift of love
That can be barely seen

For neither lamp can light the way,
Each but a flick'ring wraith,
Each glowing only for to say:
All journeys end in faith.

A Game I Never Understood

*THE RANCHER
speaks*

Fact is, as I'm recollectin',
They were much the same:
Quiet, calm, and unsuspectin',
Both playin' a game
I never fully understood.

Hired men never care
What goes to make their paycheck good
Long as they can wear
Their spare time like a Sunday suit,
All the while the boss
Must play the banker's prostitute,
Worryin' each loss
Of market, grass, and circumstance,
Knowin' all the while
His cowboys' lives is all romance
With a free-rein style.

And her, that pencil took her time.
Inbetween the chores
She fretted meter, word, and rhyme
More than whether stores
Of our comestibles were stocked
Or our larder laid
To full, so if the road was blocked
To town, we'd have stayed
Supplied with our necessities.

True, we'd not run short
Of verses for her poetries,
No way of the sort.
And yet, after the big grass fire
That near burned us out,
It was like preachin' to the choir,
Didn't take no clout
To make my dream-eyed wife decide
That supplies was down,
So long as my cowboy 'd ride
With her into town.

THE COWBOY
sings

One Breath Away From the Fire

By night, Orion wore a cloak
The moon, a flannel gown;
The prairie was a sea of smoke,
The stars, a dirty brown;
Cinders flew like autumn leaves,
Higher and higher,
One breath away from the fire.
One breath away from the fire.

Dinner-time, a lightnin' bolt
Had set the range ablaze.
The wind got up, that's all she wrote;
We saved what we could save.
Fought the flames all afternoon,
Hot, scared, and tired,
One breath away from the fire.
One breath away from the fire.

The boss had gone to Clarendon
And left his wife alone,
So, first I could, I took a run
To see about their home,
Fearin' for that helpless girl
And what might transpire
One breath away from the fire.
One breath away from the fire.

I spurred my mount across the draw
And up onto the plains,
Horrified at what I saw
Outlined against the flames:
His young wife as she saddled-up,
Her circumstances dire,
One breath away from the fire.
One breath away from the fire.

By the time I made the gate
She had her pony forked.
We struck a lope towards the breaks
And held a steady course.
She pushed her reins and stayed her tree
Like a barb on a wire,
One breath away from the fire.
One breath away from the fire.

Into a scalded wash, we dropped
And threw our horses free.
I laid above 'er 'tween the rocks
To shield her from the heat,
Doin' what I had to do
When doin' was required,
One breath away from the fire.
One breath away from the fire.

Thunder roared above the blast
And soon we felt the rain;
And though the danger, it was past,
She held me just the same,
A fearful tremble in her heart
That felt most like desire,
One breath away from the fire.
One breath away from the fire.

Ashes, After Fire

THE RANCHER
speaks

I've seen the bluestem, stirrup-deep,
Become a blackened pyre,
A wasteland, buried in the heap
Of ashes, after fire.

The old, dead grass goes up in smoke,
The wind howls in the wire,
What was, is gone, deep in the cloak
Of ashes, after fire.

Yet quick, so quick, the ranges wear
Their spanking new attire,
As tender grass grows in the care
Of ashes, after fire.

Though alchemists have lost their call
Their magics still inspire
Gold seekers in the grimy pall
Of ashes, after fire.

The Queen of the Plains

Above the River of the Arms of God
Once she played, fingering the sanded sod,
Holding it like a whisper grips a face
In seduction. Once nakedly she trod

In every open, every secret place
Without impediment and without trace
Upon this wild and level-sighted plain
Among her faceless lovers, where her grace

Was written in the flying of the crane
In paragraphs across her pale domain.
This was before the fence, before the plow,
Before the desecration of the rain,

Before the scriven eye and knotted brow
And muttered curse and twisted fist that now
Her invocation and her herald make;
When her moon was a solemn, holy vow

Demanding fealty, when the rattlesnake
And owl her sacred work would undertake,
When coyote-howl and snorting buffalo
Would rend the air and cause the prairie shake

And shiver with her prayers, and when the snow
Before her silvered feet would swirl and blow
To waltzes whirling wonderfully proud.
Invisible, impossible to know

Was she, or call her quiet name aloud,
Foolish to stand before her face unbowed,
Dangerous to make measure and to plumb
The depth and reaches of her thundercloud

Heart, in like part crazy to cower, dumb
And blind, in worship of a science numb
To the raw stroke of her power. When the night
Was her fierce bower, the days in waves would come:

First, tansy mustard, algerita bright,
Then prairie lantern with its lipid light,
Blue-eyed grass and cholla and prickly-pear,
Then gaping devil's claw and boneset, white

With healing kiss, and, last, broomweed to bear
The torch of immolation for her fair
King's funeral pyre, when her orange tongue
Licked all around his body, brown and bare,

Raced up and down his length and breadth and sung
Songs terrible to hear, her black breath flung
In ragged clouds o'er his withering fire,
Those days when death the ancient year made young.

Trembling and erect, every green-strung lyre
Breathed her hungry touch, before our barbed-wire
In its industrial, diligent crime
Martyred her music and that age entire

When reason was no art, when the sublime
Could only be known in the rustling rhyme
Of the poetry of a woman-god.
There was that time, I swear, there was that time.

In the Beginning

THE RANCHER'S
WIFE *speaks*

How will we make our first approach,
The honest thing that binds the eye
With clarity, its newness plashed
To wake the mind and rear us up
Like blinking owls on fencepost nights
Whose snare-drum hearts beat bold tattoos:
Who is it there? Who goes there? Who?

THE RANCHER
comments

Who? Who? Who? My fanny, who! And when!
It warn't no owl,
Out on the prowl,
It were a coyote, lookin' for a hen!

First, Fire

THE COWBOY
speaks

I serve in her divinity.
She is a woman, and therefore
A goddess of that trinity
Which poets pray to comprehend:
First, fire, then water, then the wind.

The first engulfs me in her glow;
The second nourishes; before
The last I rattle, shake, and blow;
Obedient unto the end
To fire, to water, and to wind.

For poets have but one true choice:
Surrender to her all their store
Of flesh and bone and soul and voice,
In trade for words which will ascend
In fire, in water, and in wind.

THE RANCHER
comments

What on earth! I don't get this poet stuff!
What's all this "goddess" bull?
I'm gettin' full
Of all this foo-fooed, mystic fluff.

THE RANCHER'S
WIFE speaks

Needlepoint

With every stitch of brightly-colored thread:
    I offer you the only thing I have;
        I take the only thing you have to give;
    I am the only thing that you can save;
        You are the only thing for which I live;
With every stitch of brightly-colored thread.

THE RANCHER
comments

Romances and riddles—there's two of a kind:
Each amuses,
Each confuses,
Each vexes, but just one of them unkind.

THE COWBOY
speaks

Come With Me

The green is on the bluestem blade—
We've finished-up the branding—
In ragged prairie colonnade
The yucca blooms are standing;
    Come with me!

The blossom's on the blue-eyed grass—
We'll wait to ride the fences—
The afternoon is free to pass
And spite the common-senses;
    Come with me!

The algerita fruit is tart
And ready for the taking—
Untie your apron, and your heart—
There's love here for the making;
    Come with me!

The Wildflower Moon

THE COWBOY
sings

When the springtime is done
And you can't stir the days with a spoon,
Our work's done
By the heat of the sun,
Our love, by the wildflower moon.

>Nights on the prairie, come summer,
>Breeze blows a beautiful tune;
>Bright are the eyes of my lover
>In the light of the wildflower moon,

Lie with me in the grass;
Stars all above us are strewn.
Let time pass
For diamonds are glass
Alongside the wildflower moon.

>Nights on the prairie, come summer,
>Breeze blows a beautiful tune;
>Bright are the eyes of my lover
>In the light of the wildflower moon,
>In the light of the wildflower moon.

THE RANCHER
comments

>At least, he's started talkin' like a man
>And not some apron-skirt,
>Though no real man would so desert
>His work in favor of a woman's hand.

Can I Be Wrong?

THE RANCHER'S
WIFE speaks

Too young, I traded all I had
Before I knew my making
And gave a promise which ignored
That hard-eyed edge of living
Which seeks more than a weary hand
Forever worn from working;
I am a woman, born of need—
Can I be wrong in wanting?

In desperation some are led
Or pushed, headlong and grasping,
To have a man without regard
To what man one is having,
But I'll not make a marriage bed
To purchase my providing;
I am a woman, grown in need—
Can I be wrong, desiring?

So soft his touch when first he held
My fingers in our courting,
His eyes that searched my every word,
His lips so shy of kissing—
How could they grow so calm and cold,
So businesslike in speaking?
I am a woman, crying need—
Can I be wrong in acting?

A Kiss Is Boundless

There is a line 'tween hurt and harmlessness,
'Tween weak and strong,
'Tween right and wrong,
But never are there boundaries to a kiss.

Those boundless kisses; how could I forget?
Now, stirred by her old poetry,
The fresh taste of their memory
Returns in breaths of glistening regret.

The Reader

I read the poetry you wrote
And felt my breath come quick
To thrill how blood so swelled my throat,
How head and tongue turned thick,
Transfixing me as if I pressed
My face against your glass,
Inhaling you as you undressed
To rhymed and metered sass
And bump and grind of phrased and lined
Voluptuary verse—

Though every garment still defined
A voyeur's silent curse,
You grew more naked as each word
Revealed your private part
To one who shamelessly preferred
That strip-tease of your heart.

Her Grant of Poetry

THE RANCHER speaks

I wish I could condemn him, but I can't.
For there is something in these words she wrote
That moves me, too. Had I enjoyed her grant
Of poetry, perhaps a wilder note
Had rung in me, perhaps I'd seen inside
The wife I had to where the woman hid.
If I had stopped to read what I denied,
I would have seen her deeper than I did.

The Mirror

THE RANCHER'S WIFE speaks

When I am told my beauty, I demure.
I own a mirror, not well-worn but used
Enough that I can say for certain sure
What I see looking back can't be confused
For beauty-queen material. My nose,
Too much my father's, has a clumsy tilt;
My eyes are shot with questions that suppose
No answers other than those sad ones built
On facts the mirror, in its truth, reflects:
This brittle, sun-bleached hair, wind-reddened skin,
Chapped lips, these crow's feet wrinkles. It detects
A blemish quicker than God sees a sin,
And never will forgive as He forgives.

Yet, when I watch your eyes as you watch me,
When ev'ry shameless, searching look relives
The first look, lingering each time to see
If there's some hidden nook or cranny yet
To be revealed, and reveled in, and when
Your lips grow soft and reverent and wet,
And when desire is open in you, then
I can my ordinariness forget
And, for a moment in your hold, deceive
Myself that my reflection in your face—
Despite what mirrors would have me believe—
Finds in me beauty, and a touch of grace.

THE RANCHER comments

> A woman who has got a man should know
> She's beautiful in his own eyes;
> He will not tell her otherwise
> But she would not be his were she not so.

The Writer

I know you're pretty. Others talk
About the glory of your walk,
The native swaying of your hips,
The crimson of your untouched lips,
The figure that you cut in silk
With breasts as bold as buttermilk
And how one wanton wisp of hair
Can lay your slender shoulders bare.
I know you're pretty. But before
I knew that, I knew something more:
I knew the labor, hard and raw,
That held your mouth and set your jaw
To penciled scribbles on the backs
Of envelopes and grocer's sacks
In careful phrases softly rolled
As ordinary cut and fold
Of daily work turned into art
By eyes that phrased a metered heart;
I read the lines that crossed the two;
I knew the poetry of you.

So if I mumble in the grip
Of tongue and lip and fingertip
Some stammered sweetnesses of how
The plunder of the here and now
Drives my desire and fires my needs
To worn-out words and fumbling deeds,
Say clichés like "you're beautiful"
And tumble on you, push and pull
The buttons, fasteners, and bows
And strip from you your weary clothes,
Set curry comb of roughened hands
To paw the coat of downy strands
That light your skin, then grope my fill
Of ev'ry touching thing until,
Your halter flung aside undone,
Turn mare and stallion out to run—
Should I surrender to the worst
Beginner's passions—know that first,
Before my blood rose hot and new,
I knew the poetry of you.

Love and Forever

THE RANCHER
speaks

It was not only him who saw her so.
I knew her first; I loved her first; I know
I never didn't love her, and so told
Her. If, perhaps, I didn't ever hold
Her like I should have held her, it was not
For lack of love. My promise that she got
Was for forever, but how many times
Must it be said, "forever," such that rhymes
And reasons of forever be believed?
Eternity—what more can be conceived
That love and obligation be made of?
Or is forever not enough for love?

To Feel Like a Lover Again

THE RANCHER'S
WIFE *sings*

Wasted and withered within
A life bereft of romance,
Waiting and hoping I'd have one more chance
To feel like a lover again.

Now, as the smell of your skin
Fingers the night in the breeze,
Here comes my memory, weak in the knees,
To feel like a lover again.

> How long has it been
> Since I felt so free?
> I'd almost forgotten how good it could be
> To feel like a lover again.

In pawn shops, old violins
Dream of the stroke of the bow
Keeping alive every song that they know
To feel like they're lovers again.

> How long has it been
> Since I felt so free?
> I'd almost forgotten how good it could be
> To feel like a lover again.

Let's don't wait to begin
To make this old feeling new;
There isn't anything I would not do
To feel like a lover again.

How long has it been
Since I felt so free?
I'd almost forgotten how good it could be
To feel like a lover again.

How long has it been
Since I felt so free?
I'd almost forgotten how good it could be
To feel like a lover again.

THE RANCHER
speaks

The Day's Stampede

I am not easy just because
I am a man. There are no laws
Of artifice or nature spun
To make of me a simpleton
Whose passion switches off and on—
Some hormone-fired automaton,
Some high-tone blooded breeding bull
Who's ever in some fanciful
Almost-aroused condition, cocked
And primed and ready, fully-stocked
To spew his pleasure at the drop
Of hint or nightgown.
                              I can't stop
The day's stampede of care: the curse
Of notes come due, the empty purse
That can't be closed to still its raw
Tongued gaping hungry bawling maw,
That can't be weaned from taking suck
By explanations of bad luck,
High costs, low prices, five-year drought.

All pretty boys soon figure out
A man is handsome in his work,
Desired for his success; the quirk
Is this: what he does to succeed
Will leave his woman in her need.

He first must do what's first in life,
Then pay attention to his wife.

And so I worked the live-long day
And worried all our nights away.

When the Devil Plays His Fiddle

THE RANCHER
speaks and sings

The tank's gone dry,
The grass is brittle,
The sand in the wind
Stings like grease from the griddle;
If it rained all day—
Too late, too little—
There's Hell to pay
When the Devil plays his fiddle.
There's Hell to pay
When the Devil plays his fiddle.

Went to the bank,
They were non-committal
But I could not beg
For the money to feed my cattle.
Curse or pray
Or stick to the middle—
There's Hell to pay
When the Devil plays his fiddle.
There's Hell to pay
When the Devil plays his fiddle.

> When the dust and sand
> Are rosin in his hands
> The high-line sings
> Like a loose bow scrapin' on the strings.

Goin' dead broke
Makes my remittal;
He carves my soul
While the good men spit and whittle.
Come what may,
Come a damn fool riddle—
There's Hell to pay
When the Devil plays his fiddle.
There's Hell to pay
When the Devil plays his fiddle.

As the Band Plays On

THE RANCHER
speaks

I am afraid to read more poetry.
My heart is torn, and not by thorn or barb
But by these words, these Godforsaken words!
What do they mean? What did they do? How far
Is love; how close deceit; how can I know?
How can I know? Where's justice in this world?

21

This could be but affection of the soul,
Or brief flirtation like a long, drawn wink
Between two strangers dancing who will squeeze
Each other's fingers when the music stops
To never meet again.
                    But what's a dance
But sex made public in a ritual
Display of courting, eye to eye and breast
To breast and loin to loin and brush of cheek
On cheek, the smell of hairspray and perfume—
My God!
            this is a dance of words, and I
Am sitting in a chair along the wall
And watching, helpless, as the band plays on.

Sonnet: To the Lost Light

I woke alone. I'd dreamed the night, in sleep
That 'round my shoulders dropped in ringlet-curls
Of emptiness, in strings of boot-black pearls
Of nothingness, my dressing-gown a deep
Unconsciousness laid bare so my desires
Lay naked to whomever else in night
Lay dreaming, too, for dark desires swell bright
And build the world at night, as night requires.
Oh! all the light of day flows from such sparks
Set loose by night, so that when night is tossed
By dreams of unanswered desire, the marks
Of moon and star and comet spin crisscrossed
In all the wild and deviled deeps and darks,
With never morning, and the light is lost.

Sonnet: The Lore of Night

I never promised anyone the moon,
Nor wished upon a star, save once or twice,
When I was young and wishes, opportune,
And promises were taken for advice.
Just one time, on a dare, I grabbed my twine
And shook a loop to throw the houlihan
To rope a comet out, but let my line
Fall slack, embarrassed by that reckless plan.
For I know little of the lore of night,
Astronomy, astrology, and such;
The black is for the lonely, and the light
Is for the lovers—I know just that much,
            And in believing what I know is true,
            I lit my lamp and fetched it here to you.

Sonnet: You Sing Too Soon

Your lamp, it has grown distant as the moon.
Behind the ringing of your spurs I hear
Your soft, sad whistle, saddling-up, a tear
Of leaving sparkling in a song whose tune
Is half lament and half hot-air balloon,
A melody part there and partly here,
The harmony of wistfulness and cheer
That every leaving brings. You sing too soon.
If you must go, at least preserve your song
Until my doorstep dwindles at your back,
Until I can no longer hear the strong
And rhythmic clip and clop and clack
Of horse-shoes hamm'ring out tattoos along
The music of your disappearing track.

*THE RANCHER'S
WIFE speaks to
The Cowboy*

Sonnet: To My Spurs

In all the clamor of the setting-out,
The noisy, busy detail that the mind
Employs to still the heart and quell that doubt
Which settles on the one who stays behind;
Within this clang of leaving, if some coy
Bejangled scrap of melody alarms
You, leads you think I sing, and sing with joy
Of going somewhere other than your arms;
You are mistaken. If you hear a song,
It is the singing of my spurs, not me.
If you hear music pulling me along
It's just those spurs a-jingle, fancy-free.
        The wishes, dreams, and prayers that sung me here
        Stand quiet now; my spurs are all we hear.

*THE COWBOY
speaks to The
Rancher's Wife*

Jingle-bob Music

There's shootin' stars pitchin' and a-buckin' tonight,
The moon is a coffee-cup porcelain white,
The river is a ribbon of silvery light,
My jingle-bob spurs ring merry and bright.

            Cottonwoods whisper
            Their soft summer song,
            Prairie grass harmonies
            Singin' along,
            An owl cries the blue notes
            A-makin' his call,
            But my jingle-bob music
            Is sweetest of all.

*THE COWBOY
sings*

The life of the cowboy is writ for the stage,
Scored in the music of bluestem and sage,
Cast for a wanderer takin' for wage
Every horizon and each turnin' page.

> Cottonwoods whisper
> Their soft summer song,
> Prairie grass harmonies
> Singin' along,
> An owl cries the blue notes
> A-makin' his call,
> But my jingle-bob music
> Is sweetest of all.

If leavin' is tragic, then stayin's a shame—
Takin' the trail, it ain't takin' the blame;
I came here singin', and I'll go the same,
Jingle-bobs ringin' the sound of her name.

> Cottonwoods whisper
> Their soft summer song,
> Prairie grass harmonies
> Singin' along,
> An owl cries the blue notes
> A-makin' his call,
> But my jingle-bob music
> Is sweetest of all.

THE RANCHER'S
WIFE speaks to
The Cowboy

Sonnet: There Is No Trail

To be with you I neither wished nor schemed;
You came to me outside my prayers. I prayed
For love, I neither for a lover laid
My supplication out, nor ever dreamed
Such heart as had a name, with blood blasphemed
By base desires, those branding fires that played
From lips to lips when my own flesh betrayed
The emptiness that from within me screamed.
By neither category nor degree
Nor name did ever I seek you, and so
It must be certain God brought you to me
And me to you, the other each to know;
Therefore, there is no trail to set you free,
And so it must be God who bids you go.

Sonnet: A Clean, Dark Brand

THE COWBOY speaks to The Rancher's Wife

This trail has no more motive than this heart.
I follow one, the other leads me on.
I take not blame or credit. When I'm gone,
Where we are now is nothing more than part
Of where we'll always be. If love's our fate,
Will we not stay in love? for love's the cross
That bears us. Love's no tally-mark of loss
Or gain, nor promise of some perfect state
Of bliss in softly-focused Kodachromes
Of Sunday morning coffees; no, my love,
Love is the waiting sky and one small dove
With miles to fly to find a coming-home.
 Of hearts and trails, all we can understand
 Is that their crossing burns a clean, dark brand.

My Cowboy Heart

THE RANCHER'S WIFE and THE COWBOY sing together

Where are you going to,
My cowboy heart?
Where the wind's blowing to,
If we must part.
Who'll read my poetry,
When I'm alone?
Vaya con Díos,
Vaquero corazón.

What was this leading to,
My cowboy heart?
I won't stop needing you
When we're apart.
Where will my passion go,
When I'm alone?
Vaya con Díos,
Vaquero corazón.

 Know, if you must go,
 My heart goes, too;
 Go, if you must go,
 And God go with you....go with you

Where are you going to,
My cowboy heart?
I won't stop loving you,
When we're apart.
Where will tomorrow go,
When I'm alone?
Vaya con Díos,
Vaquero corazón.

The Red-Tail Hawk

I know what lifts the red-tail hawk,
What pumps the thunderstorm,
What snaps the thistle at its stalk,
And how the hoo-doos form;

I know what whips the playa lake,
What spins the windmill fan,
What dunes the dust, what drifts the flake,
And how the howl began;

I know what gathers up to blow
What gives the grass to bend—
I know these things, yet I'll not know
What reason has of wind.

I know what whirls and dances me,
What fancy turns my eye,
What little things add up to be,
And how the soul can fly;

I know what in me wants the touch,
What aches in the embrace,
What excess never is too much,
And how to measure grace;

I know what gathers up to show
What fragile stuff we're of—
I know these things, yet I'll not know
What reason has of love.

Of wind or love, what reason has
I will not ever know—
Not why, not whether, not whereas;
Yet where they go, I go.

The Circle

Each gift has got two parts, two mysteries:
The first is that it comes
Unbidden and unearned and undeserved;
As such, gifts can't be kept
In greed, but must be given all away—
The second mystery.

This gift I have received: to see the world
As lovers see the world.
And though the giver of the gift is gone,
My world remains that world
That lovers see. I cry,
But am not sad, for I will make my life
The circle of the gift.

The Spirits of these Words

I know the gift I need:
I need to know the truth.
                  No! I demand
To know the truth, the bold reality
Of what they did, the two of them.
                      Details!
Regardless of how sordid or how mean
Such knowledge might be proved to be,
                        or hurt,
How badly it might hurt to know such truth!
For how can there be justice without truth,
And how can there be truth without the facts?

They are not here, except within
The spirits of these words;
I cannot ask the questions
For the answers I must have;
I cannot argue, or condemn,
Or blame, or criticize,
Or punish,

Or forgive.

THE RANCHER'S WIFE speaks as The Cowboy leaves

THE RANCHER speaks

The Price of Tea in China

In life's lesson
Love's the question,
Answers come and go;
Nothin's certain,
Then, I'm just guessin';
Do I really want to know?

> What's the price of tea in China?
> How far is too far to go?
> Were those stars in her eyes, shinin'?
> Do I really want to know?
> Do I really want to know?

Facts seem missin'
When there's somethin'
That the facts could show;
When I'm wishin'
I had seen it comin',
Do I really want to know?

> What's the price of tea in China?
> How far is too far to go?
> Were those stars in her eyes, shinin'?
> Do I really want to know?
> Do I really want to know?

Have I trusted
Once too often;
Do I catch on slow?
Is it justice,
Or just talkin';
Do I really want to know?

> What's the price of tea in China?
> How far is too far to go?
> Were those stars in her eyes, shinin'?
> Do I really want to know?
> Do I really want to know?
> What's the price of tea in China?

The Curve and Valley

Let me begin with what I know to be.
My wife
She was, and my cowboy was he.
They wrote
These poems, these romantic provocations.
He was the best cowboy I ever had.
The only love I ever had was she.
He stayed two years, then left before the fall.
And death took her from me.

He left before the fall; she never said
His name again,
but in the spring she bore
A son, a son whom we have raised...
My God!
Our only child!
Can it be
I'm a bull whose get was but one calf
In thirty years?
Is my seed lacking flower?

Who does he look like?
Me,
Or him?
Has he my eyes,
Or his?
If he knew what I know right now,
Would he call me
"Father"?

For she and I have had
Sweet opportunities. When we
Were courting, we could not keep
Ourselves unto ourselves.
We were young,
Naive,
But eager to explore
And quick to learn.

And what about our honeymoon?
We took my daddy's Oldsmobile
To Lubbock to the Hilton
For three days' room service,
Never even walked next door
To see a matinee.

Oh, my!
We made up sights we'd seen
To tell the folks back home
When they inquired
Did we have fun.

And then...
One evening, in the fall after the cowboy left,
I found her standing silent on this porch.
The setting sun had set her hair aglow
And framed an amber halo 'round her head
And scattered embers in a mist around her shape
And shone right through the cotton dress she wore.
I called her name, and, when she turned her face,
Her eyes were round and wet
And she stood silent, still,
The sunset orange neon tear stains shining
'Til I kissed them dry,
The salty taste of her that made me hungry
For the rest of her, her lips,
Her skin, her hair, the curve and valley
Of her, all of her.

Daybreak woke us, still upon the porch
In one another's arms, the dogs at play
With dress and trouser, boots and shoes.

We laughed all afternoon at being stiff and sore
From these hard boards.

We have had opportunities
For other children,
For more than the one,

So ours must not be ours,
But theirs.

What will I tell
This son that I have raised?

The truth. I have no other choice.
I will tell my...

I will tell her son the truth.

The Moon of Giving Birth

THE RANCHER
speaks

It was the time of year for flowers when he came;

THE RANCHER'S
WIFE *takes up the
poem*

The time of year the grass had gone to green;
The time of year when anvil thunderheads, aflame
With yellows, oranges, and pinks, pristine
In whitest whites, grew pregnant with the freshened rain,
Grew heavy-bellied blue; the thirsty earth
Awaiting and impatient for the rite of pain,
That time of year, the moon of giving birth.

It was the time of year for flowers,

THE RANCHER
resumes the poem

Wild along the barrow-ditches and the road-cuts up the Cap Rock:
Swelling dusty clouds of yellow tall sweet-clover rimmed with green
Alfalfa, purple-flecked, with crazy-weed shot through,
And bashful cowboy roses stuck amidst the Indian blankets,
Brassy-bright against their kin—sunflowers fencepost tall,
Short blackweed asters, zinnias, daisies—
All flirtatious underneath a paintbrush sky;
The time of year for algerita, too, its early fruit
Blood-red but hard as flint, for purple lavender,
For buffalo burrs, for Texas thistles soft yet for the spring.

It was the time of year for flowers when he came,
When all the world is made of growing things,
When all the sky grows higher with the standing sun,
That time of year, the moon of first-born sons.

The Future In the Child

THE RANCHER'S
WIFE *speaks*

A child is of its mother's flesh
And of its father's name,
And though each love it just as much,
They love it not the same.

A baby is a mother's joy

THE RANCHER
continues the poem

No father understands.
But let it grow to girl or boy
And then 'tis father's hands

That lead the children out of doors

THE RANCHER'S
WIFE *continues the
poem*

And give them leave to roam
To foreign lands and foreign shores,
Away from hearth and home,

For mother is the cradle's ease
That holds her baby mild,
But while she rocks, the father sees
The future in the child.

A Prairie Mother's Prayer

He's so small,
Such a tiny thing;
He needs my all,
He needs everything that is dear
In a mother's care,
So, God, please hear his prairie mother's prayer:

> Let him bend
> Before the wind,
> Lift him up
> When he's laid low,
> Let a thunderstorm
> His spirit form,
> Fill his cup
> With rain and snow,
> Let him green his days
> As seasons pass,
> Let him grow I pray
> The way of the grass.

At my breast,
He is innocence;
His life is blessed
With the sacred sense of the gift,
And there's none so fair
As a baby with his prairie mother's prayer.

> Let him bend
> Before the wind,
> Lift him up
> When he's laid low,
> Let a thunderstorm
> His spirit form,
> Fill his cup
> With rain and snow,
> Let him green his days
> As seasons pass,
> Let him grow I pray
> The way of the grass.

32

Fathers pray
That their sons grow strong,
Come what may,
Come to right or wrong; mothers live
What their babies bear
And so I give this prairie mother's prayer:

> Let him bend
> Before the wind,
> Lift him up
> When he's laid low,
> Let a thunderstorm
> His spirit form,
> Fill his cup
> With rain and snow,
> Let him green his days
> As seasons pass,
> Let him grow I pray
> The way of the grass.

In Faith and Blood

THE RANCHER
speaks

The way of grass? the way of grass? how grows
The grass? And is that how a child grows up?
For we aren't called to raise the grass; grass knows
Its green faith rises in the spilling cup

Of rain and snow, in sunlight's whiskey breath,
So seeks no answers from the earth, this grass,
But makes its silent push a shibboleth
For birth, and life, and death, and all that pass

Unnoticed in this world on its round turn.
But diff'rent from all other growing things,
The child is formed of question, and must learn
What information can discern, what rings

Of fact, the ordinary things we know,
The solid evidence that will endure,
Details we cannot doubt, the things that show
A puzzle, yes, but rational and sure.

I taught him how to ride, and how to rope,
How horses think, and all the cattle lore
Passed down to me by my own father's scope
Of common sense, and all the gathered store

Of educated plunder that is got
By working side-by-side with old cowhands:
When dally welters work, and when a knot
Tied hard and fast is best; the names of brands

And how to smear one on; to watch the moon
To know what time is right to geld the colt;
To mind the slack, but don't pull slack too soon;
To pray for rain, but fear the thunderbolt;

That easy reins will make an easy ride;
That good experience will see him through;
That work is more than labor dignified;
That he would have to trust to what he knew.

One moonless midnight, January late,
The north wind slinging sleet with sting and slap,
The boy and I, he was just turning eight,
Were checking first-calf heifers in a trap

Below the canyon rim, far from this place,
And found a cow whose calf was coming turned.
Both weakened from the strain, this was a case
To get some help, which I most always spurned

At calvin' time. It so required I stayed,
As we'd already three calves to attend,
Therefore I sent the boy. He was afraid;
The way could not be seen. Into the wind

I pointed him, told him to spur his horse
And give the brute his head; when on the rim
To watch for light, then ride a steady course
And don't turn 'round; and I reminded him,

Before I slapped his mount and sent him pack,
I 'minded him about the coal-oil lamp
His mother lit to guide us safely back.
Then, as he disappeared into the damp

Ice crystal night, he turned and looked at me,
With neither doubt nor question in his eyes,
Still scared, but all the man a boy could be.
In faith and blood, there is no compromise.

Washed In The Flood

THE RANCHER
sings

With argument, you analyze
Worries you will agonize,
But truth has got no alibis
In faith and blood, there is no compromise.

> Washed in the flood
> Each sanctifies;
> There is faith, there is blood,
> There is no compromise.

Reason swears and testifies
That this one's that one in disguise,
But casting lots, it purifies
In faith and blood, there is no compromise.

> Washed in the flood
> Each sanctifies;
> There is faith, there is blood,
> There is no compromise.

The rush of faith, it mystifies
The rising blood, it glorifies
The heart and soul, for each arise
In faith and blood, there is no compromise.

> Washed in the flood
> Each sanctifies;
> There is faith, there is blood,
> There is no compromise.

The Gift

THE RANCHER
speaks

Though I can never hold my wife again,
I have her poetry, I have our son,
And ever if I feel that lick of pain,
The doubt of what was done, or wasn't done,

I'll nothing need but this: faith is the gift
The heart makes from that truth that can't be bound
By facts; should ever we be set adrift,
It is the lamp that burns to make us found.

The Windmill Lamp

When the way is strange
On your pilgrim tramp
Through the night of worry and care,
On a windmill hangs
A burning lamp
Shining light that will lead you there.

> Far away, the lamp will guide you;
> All the way, the love that's true;
> Go your way, the faith inside you,
> It's the gift, it's meant for you;
> Take the gift, it's meant for you.

While the windmill turns
High upon its tower
Lifting water up from the ground
There are lips that burn
All the awful hours
Of the lost way seeking the found.

> Far away, the lamp will guide you;
> All the way, the love that's true;
> Go your way, the faith inside you,
> It's the gift, it's meant for you;
> Take the gift, it's meant for you.

You may never know
Who has kept the flame,
Or whose hand hung the lamp so high;
Yet its simple glow
It is just the same
As the sun that lights all the sky.

> Far away, the lamp will guide you;
> All the way, the love that's true;
> Go your way, the faith inside you,
> It's the gift, it's meant for you;
> Take the gift, it's meant for you.

A Few Terms

dally welters—in roping from horseback, to secure the rope to the saddle horn by wrapping the rope around the horn after the throw is made, as opposed to **tied hard-and-fast**, in which the rope has been tied to the saddle horn prior to the throw

forty and found—how a cowboy described his pay: forty dollars a month and "found," which amounted to room and board in the bunkhouse or at the wagon

to have your pony forked—to be mounted horseback

hoo-doo—a geologic formation common in the canyons of the southwest, a spire of earth cut away from the canyon walls by erosion, standing alone and capped with a rock or hard strata

houlihan (or hooley-ann)—a quick, overhand rope throw, often done afoot

jingle-bob spurs—spurs on which small bits of metal have been affixed to the outside hub of the spur rowell for decoration and for the pleasant sound. The name comes from their resemblance to a particular method of marking a calf's ears during branding, also called a jinglebob cut, in which a deep slit left the bottom half of the ear flapping down.

segundo—the second in command

smear one on—to rope

ABOUT THE RECORDING

The accompanying compact disk recording contains the following songs:

1 The Tribe of the Forty and Found *The Cowboy*
2 Do You Know My Name? *The Rancher's Wife*
3 One Breath Away From the Fire *The Cowboy and The Rancher's Wife*
4 The Wildflower Moon *The Cowboy*
5 To Feel Like a Lover Again *The Rancher's Wife*
6 When the Devil Plays His Fiddle *The Rancher*
7 Jingle-bob Music *The Cowboy*
8 My Cowboy Heart *The Rancher's Wife and The Cowboy*
9 The Price of Tea in China *The Rancher*
10 A Prairie Mother's Prayer *The Rancher's Wife*
11 Washed in the Flood *The Rancher*
12 The Windmill Lamp *The Rancher, The Rancher's Wife, and The Cowboy*

The original cast members perform on this recording:
Don Allison as The Cowboy;
Kenny Maines as The Rancher;
Lesley Sawyer as The Rancher's Wife.

Lloyd Maines produced the music.
George Sorensen directed the play.

The musicians are:
Lloyd Maines, guitars;
Richard Bowden, fiddle;
Joe Carr, mandolin and fiddle;
Ed Marsh, bass and fiddle;
Alan Munde, banjo.

The music was recorded at Grey Horse Studio, Lubbock, TX, and mixed at Crystal Creek Studios, Austin, TX and Brazos Studios, Lubbock, TX

All songs were written by Andy Wilkinson, © Cain't Quit Music, Inc./BMI 1998.